Everything You Need to Know About

Anemia

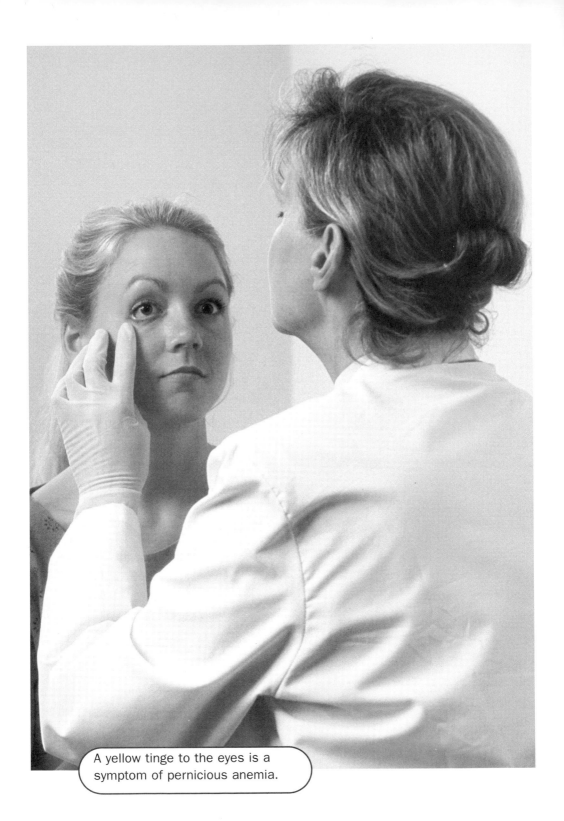

A yellow tinge to the eyes is a symptom of pernicious anemia.

Everything You Need to Know About

Anemia

Allison J. Ross

The Rosen Publishing Group, Inc.
New York

Published in 2000 by The Rosen Publishing Group, Inc.
29 East 21st Street, New York, NY 10010

First Edition

Library of Congress Cataloging-in-Publication Data

Ross, Allison J., 1974–
    Everything you need to know about anemia / Allison J. Ross
      p. cm.—(The need to know library)
    Includes bibliographical references and index.
    Summary: Discusses the various types of anemia, as well as its causes, symptoms, treatment, and preventative measures.
    ISBN 0-8239-3218-4
      1. Anemia—Juvenile literature. [1. Anemia] I. Title II. Series.

RC641.R67 2000
616.1'52—dc21   00-024825

Manufactured in the United States of America

Contents

Introduction

Do you have anemia or know someone who does? Anemia is the most common disorder of the red blood cells, so it is quite likely that you have at least heard of the disease. What you may not know is what causes anemia, how it makes you feel, and who is at risk. But before we get into that, let's discuss what anemia means.

To begin with, it is helpful to know that the blood circulating in our bodies is made up of red blood cells (yellowish disk-shaped blood cells that contain hemoglobin) and white blood cells (white or colorless nucleated cells). Our blood also has platelets, which help the blood to clot, and plasma, the liquid part of the blood. Plasma contains various nutrients and proteins.

So what does all of this have to do with anemia? As previously mentioned, anemia is a disorder of the red blood cells. Inside the red blood cells is a colored agent, or pigment, called hemoglobin. Hemoglobin is responsible for carrying the oxygen that we breathe. Anemia occurs when the amount of hemoglobin in the blood is less than what is needed to carry oxygen to all of the cells in your body. That sounds simple enough, but what makes anemia a little more complicated is the fact that there are many forms of the disease—in fact, there are more than four hundred different types. Also, many of the different types of anemia have different causes. For example, some types of anemia are caused by improper nutrition, whereas others are inherited.

You may be wondering how you know if you have anemia. Although there are hundreds of different types of anemia, many of the symptoms of the disease are the same: weakness and general fatigue, and paleness of the skin, gums, eyes, and nail beds. In more severe incidences, an anemic person may notice heart palpitations and shortness of breath.

If you experience any of these symptoms, you should make an appointment to see a doctor. The only way to know for sure if you have anemia—and what type of anemia you have—is to have your doctor do a physical exam and run tests on a sample of your blood. It is important that you get an official diagnosis so that, if necessary, you can begin a treatment program.

This book will tell you all you need to know about anemia, so read on.

Anemia can cause severe fatigue
even in normally energetic people.

Chapter One

Anemia— What Is It?

*J*anice was always full of energy. As a ninth grader, she stayed busy doing homework and hanging out with her friends. Janice was also a member of a community-service club, and she played the flute in the school band. On top of all of that, she was the captain of her soccer team.

About halfway through the school year, Janice began noticing that she was more tired than usual. Also, she was frequently out of breath during soccer practice. But Janice was so busy with all of her various activities, she did not really have a chance to pay much attention to how she was feeling.

Then one day in December, Janice's mother noticed that her daughter did not look well. She was pale and had large dark circles under her eyes. She also seemed far less energetic than usual. Mrs. O'Malley thought that Janice should go and see the doctor to make sure that everything was okay. Janice thought her mother was being a little too cautious, and at first she would not agree to go.

"You are being very unreasonable, Janice," said Mrs. O'Malley. "All I want you to do is go for a simple checkup. It's not like I'm asking you to pull out your teeth."

"But, Mom, you are just overreacting. I mean, I may be a bit pale, but that's because I haven't been at the beach since July."

"Look, dear, I am just going to make the appointment, and you will just have to go. Your health is very important. And that's the end of this conversation."

In the end, Janice went to the doctor. And in fact, the visit with the doctor was pretty simple.

Dr. Ramos asked Janice some questions about her health and eating habits, and he did a physical exam. At the end of the exam, he took a blood sample from Janice's arm. He told Janice he would call her when the results came back from the laboratory. A couple of days later, Janice's doctor called, and she went to see him again. The results from the blood test showed that Janice had a mild form of iron-deficiency anemia. Fortunately, it wasn't too serious, and Janice and her doctor were able to come up with a plan to correct the anemia. This plan included taking daily iron *supplements and eating iron-rich foods, such as green, leafy vegetables.*

Shortly after she began her new diet, Janice went back to the doctor for a follow-up blood test. The test revealed that Janice's iron levels were normal, and Janice felt great.

Iron-Deficiency Anemia

As you just read, maintaining an adequate supply of iron in our bodies is very important. But why? For one thing, iron is used by the body to manufacture hemoglobin, which carries oxygen to the cells of the body. So if your body doesn't have enough iron, it won't make enough hemoglobin. This will lead to iron-deficiency anemia.

Do you know where our bodies keep the iron we take in? You may be surprised to learn that our bodies reserve iron in our bone marrow, liver, and spleen. When we eat foods that contain large amounts of iron, the iron in our bodies is replenished. Also, when the red blood cells break down, the iron in them is recycled. The most common type of anemia is iron-deficiency anemia. Iron-deficiency anemia occurs when the body doesn't have enough iron, or is iron deficient.

Signs and Symptoms

If you feel weak, tired, and you just generally don't feel well, you may have iron-deficiency anemia. You may also notice one or all of the following symptoms: bluish lips; pasty or yellow skin; pale gums, nail beds, eyelid linings, and palm creases. If you also frequently feel out of breath and feel faint or dizzy, you may have severe anemia.

Causes

This disorder occurs much more often in women than in men. In fact, in the United States, 20 percent of all women of childbearing age have iron-deficiency anemia—compared to only 2 percent of adult men. This may seem a little strange, but there's an easy explanation. Iron-deficiency anemia is caused by a lack of iron reserves. Because iron is lost when we bleed, the primary cause of iron-deficiency anemia is menstruation. The blood that is lost during menstruation causes women to lose valuable amounts of iron. Even women who have normal menstrual bleeding can deplete, or use up, their iron reserves over a period of months. This is why so many more women than men have iron-deficiency anemia. You may also lose a lot of blood from another medical condition, such as a peptic ulcer, polyp of the colon, cancer of the stomach or intestine, or hemorrhoids. These problems may also cause iron-deficiency anemia.

Aside from bleeding, another cause of iron-deficiency anemia is diet. If you eat too few iron-rich foods, or don't absorb enough iron, you may be at risk for this form of anemia. Although the recommended daily allowance (RDA) for iron ranges from 6 milligrams for infants to 30 milligrams for pregnant women, females between the ages of twelve and fifty years old get about half of what they need. Iron reserves can also be depleted in women who are pregnant or breast-feeding, and older women with poor diets may develop the disorder as well.

Who Is at Risk?

In addition to older women and women who are pregnant or are breast-feeding, children are also at risk for iron-deficiency anemia. The three pediatric age groups most at risk for this type of anemia are infants, toddlers, and adolescents. Infants are at risk if they were born prematurely or at a low birth weight, or if their mothers did not get enough iron when they were pregnant. Toddlers are at risk for iron-deficiency anemia if they don't establish healthy eating habits and eat enough of the right foods.

As we saw in Janice's case, adolescents are a particularly high-risk group for iron deficiency. The combination of the extra iron requirements of the growth spurt, poor eating habits, and, in females, the onset of menstruation, all combine to produce a high risk of iron deficiency. Because of these factors, 9 percent of all females are iron deficient, compared to only 2 percent of males.

Treatment and Prevention

Treatment for iron-deficiency anemia depends on what the specific cause is. For example, if the cause of your iron deficiency is a lack of iron in your diet, then perhaps an iron supplement is all that you need to help correct your condition. On the other hand, if a person has anemia because of an ulcer, the treatment will be more complex. In this case, the ulcer must be treated before the anemia can be properly taken care of.

If you think you may have anemia, you should see your doctor. He or she will be able to make an official diagnosis and will know best how to treat you. Your treatment may include some or all of the following:

- Eat more foods that are good sources of iron. Some of these include green, leafy vegetables; lean red meat; beef; liver; poultry; fish; wheat germ; oysters; dried fruit; and iron-fortified cereals.

- Boost your iron absorption by eating foods high in vitamin C. Citrus fruits, tomatoes, and strawberries help your body to absorb iron from food. Also, red meat can increase your absorption of iron from other food sources.

- Limit your tea consumption. Tea contains tannins, which can inhibit iron absorption. Herbal tea, however, is okay to drink.

- Take an iron supplement. Consult your physician for the proper dosage (this is very important, as recent research suggests that high

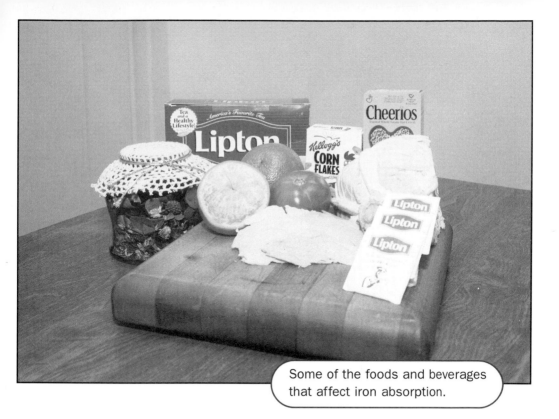

Some of the foods and beverages that affect iron absorption.

levels of iron in the blood may increase the risk for heart attacks). Also, although iron is best absorbed taken on an empty stomach, it can upset your stomach. Thus, it's best to take iron with meals.

- Avoid antacids and phosphates (which are found in soda, ice cream, and candy bars). These all block iron absorption.

- Increase dietary fiber to prevent constipation.

Folic-Acid Deficiency

Iron-deficiency anemia isn't the only common form of anemia. Another type is folic-acid deficiency anemia (or megaloblastic anemia). Just as low levels of iron cause

15

iron-deficiency anemia, folic-acid deficiency occurs when there are low levels of folic acid.

Folic acid is important, and it offers many health benefits. Among other things, folic acid is necessary for the normal maturation of red blood cells, and it helps protect your chromosomes. It also promotes healthier skin and helps keep you from getting food poisoning. Also, recent studies show that folic acid in high doses can help protect people from cardiovascular disease.

Signs and Symptoms

If you have folic-acid deficiency anemia, you may experience some of the following symptoms: loss of appetite, diarrhea, a tingling and/or numbness in the hands and feet, pale skin color, tiredness, headaches, sore mouth and tongue, and/or jaundice. If a pregnant woman does not get enough folic acid, her baby is at risk for being born with a low birth weight and neural tube defects. Also, folic-acid deficiency can lead to infertility and an increased risk of infection.

Causes

Usually, the cause of folic-acid deficiency is inadequate dietary intake, which means that you don't get enough folic acid through what you eat. Another cause is faulty absorption, which occurs when your body doesn't properly absorb the folic acid you take in. Pregnant women need more than twice the normal amount of folic acid,

Folic-acid deficiency anemia can cause tiredness and loss of appetite, among other things.

so they usually take a folic acid supplement of 400 micrograms (mcg) to 1 milligram (mg) per day.

Who Is at Risk?

Drinking alcohol interferes with the metabolism of folic acid, so folic-acid deficiency anemia is often seen in people who drink a lot of alcohol. It can also occur in patients with cancer, celiac disease (a malabsorption problem), and other disorders. Older women often have a deficiency in this vitamin, especially those with poor diets. As previously mentioned, pregnant women are also at risk.

Treatment and Prevention

As with iron-deficiency anemia, it is important to consult

your doctor for a proper diagnosis and treatment plan. Because folic-acid deficiency anemia strongly resembles another type of anemia (called pernicious anemia, to be discussed in the next chapter), careful diagnostic tests must be performed by your doctor to distinguish between the two.

To get and make the best use of folic acid, your doctor may recommend that you do some or all of the following:

- Eat good food sources of folic acid daily. You can find folic acid in vegetables like asparagus, brussels sprouts, spinach, romaine lettuce, collard greens, and broccoli. Other good sources include black-eyed peas, cantaloupe, orange juice, oatmeal, whole grain cereals, wheat germ, and liver.

- Eat fresh, uncooked fruits and vegetables. Because heat destroys folic acid, make sure you don't overcook your food.

- Take a multivitamin supplement daily that has 100 percent of the recommended daily allowance (RDA) for folic acid.

Folic-acid deficiency can be corrected with a change in diet and folic acid supplements (either injected or given orally), so the prognosis for people undergoing treatment for this disorder is good.

Chapter Two

Pernicious Anemia

In addition to the more common types of anemia that were described in the first chapter, there are also rarer forms of the disease. One of these is pernicious anemia, which is sometimes called Addison's anemia or vitamin B-12 deficiency.

If you have pernicious anemia, this means that your body does not have enough vitamin B-12. Vitamin B-12 is found only in foods of animal origin, such as meat, fish, and dairy products. Because B-12 is readily available in meats and is easily stored in the liver, most healthy nonvegetarians have a three- to five-year reserve in their bodies.

If vitamin B-12 is so readily available in the foods we eat, then why don't some people get enough vitamin B-12? The answer is that vitamin B-12 deficiency is generally not caused by a lack of vitamin B-12, but rather by a

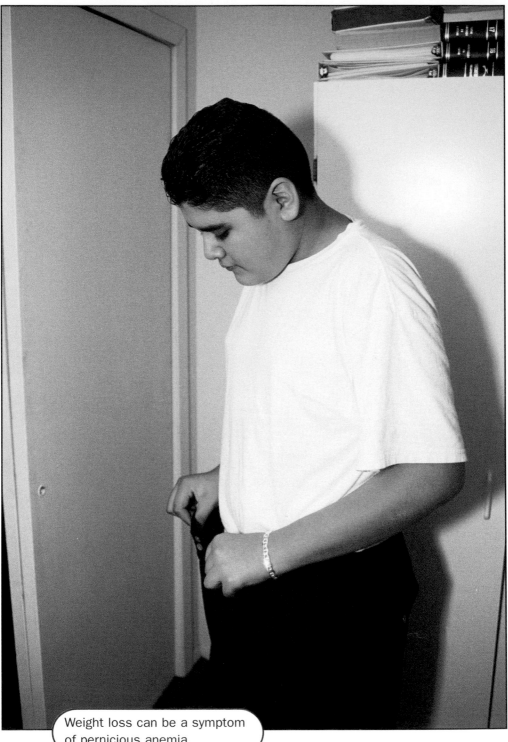

Weight loss can be a symptom of pernicious anemia.

failure to absorb the vitamin through the digestive tract. In other words, although you may be eating enough foods with vitamin B-12, your body isn't absorbing it properly.

Kevin's Complications from Surgery

When Kevin was twenty-two, he had minor stomach surgery. It was a relatively quick procedure, and Kevin was allowed to go home from the hospital after a couple of days. Fortunately, his recovery went well, and he was back at work in no time.

A few months later, Kevin noticed that he did not feel right. Even though he had been eating a lot, his pants started to feel loose. He thought that maybe he was losing weight. He soon began to notice other problems, too. His skin was looking a little yellow, and his stomach hurt. Kevin called Dr. Samuel, who was his doctor and surgeon. When Kevin had the surgery, Dr. Samuel had mentioned that he was at risk for something called pernicious anemia. Pernicious anemia means that the body does not have enough vitamin B-12. According to Dr. Samuel, sometimes people who have had stomach surgery are at risk for developing the disease. Kevin made an appointment to see his doctor right away.

As it turned out, Dr. Samuel's assumption was right. Because of the surgery, Kevin's body was not producing enough hydrochloric acid. This was making it hard for his body to properly absorb vit-amin B-12.

Signs and Symptoms

The symptoms of pernicious anemia develop slowly and gradually, and may not be immediately recogniz-able. Some of the signs and symptoms that are associ-ated with the disease are weakness and tiredness, intermittent (not constant) constipation and diarrhea, abdominal pain, bleeding gums, nausea, appetite loss and weight loss, sore tongue, yellowish tinge to the eyes and skin, and a shortness of breath.

Certain neurological signs may also be present with per-nicious anemia, including tingling sensations in the hands and feet, difficulty in balance, and a lack of coordination.

Causes

Pernicious anemia can be caused by an improper diet, esp-ecially a vegetarian diet lacking vitamin B-12, and a diet without supplements. Also, people with a vitamin B-12 deficiency often lack a substance called intrinsic factor. Intrinsic factor is normally secreted by the stomach and makes absorption of vitamin B-12 possible. If you do not have intrinsic factor, your body will not be able to properly process vitamin B-12. We do not know why some people are missing intrinsic factor, but it may be a genetic defi-ciency or the result of an autoimmune disorder .

Intrinsic factor is not the only substance that makes vitamin B-12 absorption possible. Hydrochloric acid is also necessary. As we saw with Kevin, sometimes people who have had stomach surgery are lacking hydrochloric acid, and this makes it difficult for their bodies to properly absorb vitamin B-12. Also, people who have had part of the stomach or intestine surgically removed, or who have a diseased ileum (a small segment of the intestine) may also be at risk for pernicious anemia.

Thyroid disorders, eating disorders (such as anorexia and bulimia), and certain genetic factors are also associated with pernicious anemia.

Who Is at Risk?

Pernicious anemia often affects adults between the ages of fifty and sixty, and usually does not appear before the age of thirty. However, a juvenile form of the disease can occur in children and is usually evident before a child is three years old. Pernicious anemia can affect all racial groups, but the incidence is higher among people of Scandinavian or northern European descent. It is found in one out of a thousand people.

Diagnosis and Treatment

If you think you may have pernicious anemia, make an appointment with your doctor. Your doctor may do a blood test and perform the Schilling's test. The

If you are diagnosed with pernicious anemia, your doctor may treat you with vitamin B-12 injections.

Schilling's test involves an injection of vitamin B-12. After the injection, the doctor measures the amount of vitamin B-12 that is in the urine. This test will reveal how well your body is absorbing vitamin B-12. Also, occasionally a bone marrow biopsy is used to confirm this disease. Although pernicious anemia is not preventable, treatment can prevent continued symptoms.

After you are diagnosed with pernicious anemia, your doctor may suggest that you receive vitamin B-12 injections. At first, you will receive the injections several times a week. After a while, however, the vitamin reserves will begin to build up in your liver, so you will need to receive the injections less often. Eventually, you may need injections only once a month, but they must be continued throughout your life.

Chapter Three

Aplastic Anemia

Another relatively rare form of anemia is called aplastic anemia. This disease occurs when the marrow does not function normally, and the production of red blood cells is dramatically reduced. If you do not have sufficient red blood cells, oxygen won't be able to reach the organs and tissues in your body.

There are two forms of aplastic anemia: primary and secondary. The cause of primary aplastic anemia is unknown and is difficult to treat. Secondary aplastic anemia, on the other hand, is more common (although still quite rare). It is usually caused by drugs or toxic substances. For example, if a person is exposed to chemical agents such as benzene and arsenic, he or she may be at risk for aplastic anemia. Similarly, if a person is exposed to radiation or many of the chemotherapeutic drugs used in cancer treatment, he or she may get secondary aplastic anemia as a result.

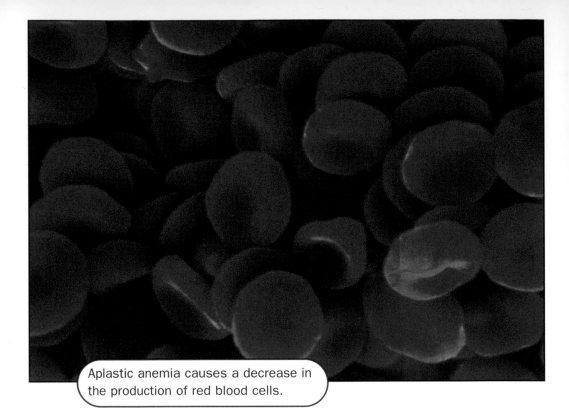

Aplastic anemia causes a decrease in the production of red blood cells.

Signs and Symptoms

Aplastic anemia generally develops slowly. As a result, you may begin to notice your symptoms only gradually. Because this form of anemia is associated with a decrease in the production of red blood cells, you will notice the usual symptoms of anemia, such as tiredness and weakness. Many of the symptoms of aplastic anemia depend on which of the cells in your body are affected. As an example, if you have a decrease in white blood cells, you may be particularly susceptible to infections. On the other hand, if you have a decrease in platelets, you will have an increased chance of spontaneous bruising and bleeding.

Causes of Aplastic Anemia

As mentioned at the beginning of this chapter, secondary aplastic anemia has been clearly linked to radiation, environmental toxins, insecticides, and drugs. Benzene-based compounds, model glue, and certain drugs have also been linked to this disease. In some individuals, aplastic anemia is believed to be caused by a virus. The exact cause of the disease in more than half the cases is unknown. Although the disease is rare, anyone can get aplastic anemia: men and women, children and adults, and people of any race and socioeconomic status.

Diagnosis

If you suspect you may have aplastic anemia, see your doctor. He or she will do a blood test to measure your blood cell levels. If your doctor finds low blood cell levels, the next step is to do an examination of a small sample of your bone marrow. A bone marrow biopsy is easily carried out in the examining room or hospital bed. To do this procedure, your doctor will insert a sturdy needle into your large pelvic bone (just beneath your belt line) on either side of your spine. This procedure may sound painful, but your doctor will give you a drug that will numb the area so that you will feel less pain during the procedure.

If you have aplastic anemia, the bone marrow biopsy will show a great reduction in the number of cells in the

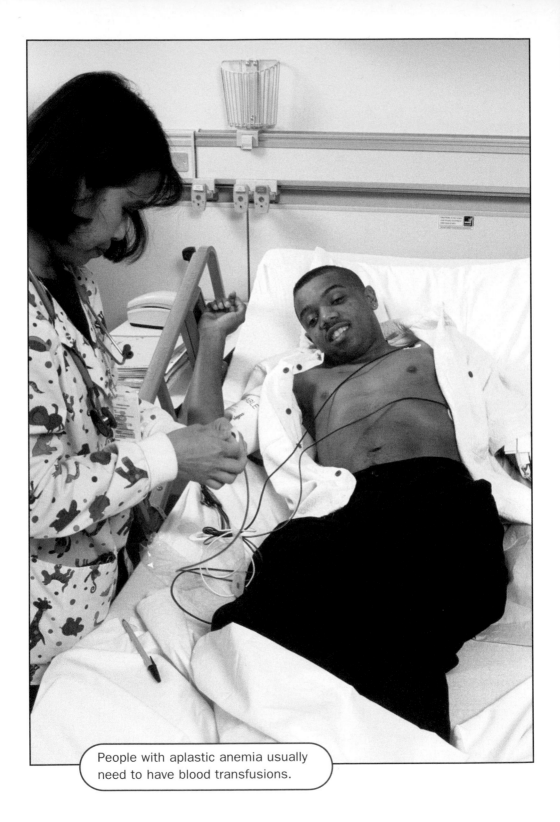

People with aplastic anemia usually need to have blood transfusions.

bone marrow, but the few remaining cells will have a normal appearance. The official diagnosis of aplastic anemia is usually made or confirmed by a specialist in blood disorders, called a hematologist.

Treatment

Because aplastic anemia is a serious disease, it is considered a medical emergency. If your case is severe, it may require immediate hospital treatment. Usually, a person with aplastic anemia will need to have blood transfusions. The transfusions are accompanied by antibiotics to combat infection. However, it is important to remember that blood transfusions are considered to be only a temporary solution to the problems of aplastic anemia patients.

In patients under age forty, bone marrow transplantation can be quite helpful. In fact, there is a possibility that you will be cured by bone marrow transplantation. If you are going to undergo this procedure, you must have a compatible donor who has bone marrow just like yours. Very often a compatible donor is an identical twin or a perfectly matched sibling. If you do not have a perfect match within your family, a search of bone marrow registries may be undertaken to find someone who would make a good donor for you.

Other forms of therapy are being used for patients who do not have a matched donor, who are more than forty years of age, or who are not good candidates for bone marrow transplantation. These include drug therapies and immunosuppressive therapies, which work with a patient's immune system. Fortunately, new therapies are being developed all the time. For this reason, make sure you talk to your doctor about the treatments that are available to you.

The prognosis of people with aplastic anemia varies, depending on the cause of the disease. For example, there is a possibility that you will be cured by bone marrow transplantation (if you are in relatively good health prior to bone marrow transplantation and you have a matched donor). In fact, more than half of good candidates for this procedure are cured by bone marrow transplantation. However, if a patient has a type of aplastic anemia for which no cause is discovered, the prognosis is poorer. About half of these patients with severe anemia will succumb to bleeding and infection within a year.

What You Can Do

There are many things you can do if you are diagnosed with aplastic anemia.

- ◆ Research all you can about your aplastic anemia and treatment options.

- ◆ Gather information from as many people as possible, including health professionals and other patients.

- Don't be afraid to ask questions from different sources until you fully understand the answers.

- Record information in a notebook. This way, you will have something to refer to and you can build on the information you have learned. You might also want to consider taking a tape recorder with you to appointments and meetings with your doctor and other health professionals.

- Encourage friends and family to become platelet and bone marrow donors.

- Join a support group and read about ways to cope with your disease. Speaking with others who have similar symptoms and questions can help you understand the disease.

You can also check with your doctor regarding some of the activities you should avoid. For example, patients with low red blood cell counts should avoid excessive exercise, being at high altitudes, or doing activities that bring on a fast heart rate, chest pain, or severe shortness of breath. If the doctor finds that you have low platelets, you should avoid activities that could result in trauma (especially head trauma). Such activities include contact sports like football and hockey.

Chapter Four

Hemolytic Anemia

Yet another rare form of anemia is hemolytic anemia (also called warm reactive antibody autoimmune hemolytic anemia, or anemia-idiopathic autoimmune hemolytic). Hemolytic anemia occurs when your red blood cells are destroyed prematurely. This type of anemia can also result if your red blood cells are broken down (hemolyzed) at a faster rate than normal.

Leonard's Trip to the Hospital

School was almost over for the day, but Leonard was so nervous he couldn't sit still. He was waiting for his mom to pick him up and take him to visit his classmate Nina, who was in the hospital. Leonard was a little afraid of hospitals, and he didn't know what to expect. What if Nina looked really sick, or what if she didn't want to see him?

When Leonard's mother arrived, she suggested that they stop at the florist to get some flowers for Nina. Leonard picked beautiful yellow roses, which were Nina's favorite. He knew the flowers would make her happy.

In the car on the way to the hospital, Leonard's mother told him about the disease Nina had, which was called hemolytic anemia. Then she explained that this condition means that the red blood cells are broken down faster than normal. Nina was in the hospital recovering from a splenectomy, or removal of the spleen. Leonard's mom said that sometimes this is necessary in the treatment of hemolytic anemia.

Leonard was still nervous when he walked into Nina's room—but all that disappeared when he saw his friend. All around Nina's bed were huge baskets of yellow roses! "I guess this wasn't the most original idea," said Leonard, handing Nina the flowers. Nina laughed. She was so glad her friend had come to visit her! And Leonard was glad that he had, too.

Signs and Symptoms

If you have hemolytic anemia, there are many symptoms you may notice or experience. Some of these are: fatigue, paleness, shortness of breath, irregular

If you have a family history of hemolytic anemia, you may be at risk.

heartbeat, jaundice, and dark urine. Also, a physical examination by your doctor may show that you have an enlarged spleen.

Causes

The cause of hemolytic anemia may be hereditary; sometimes a hereditary condition called spherocytosis causes the red blood cells to be broken down faster than normal. Hemolytic anemia can also be caused by the presence of antibodies in the blood that attack the red cells, drugs taken for other conditions, or a variety of disorders (such as sickle-cell anemia and thalassemia, which will be discussed in the next chapter).

In some cases, the cause is not known, and therefore there is no known prevention for the disease. The onset may be quite rapid and can be very serious. Because hemolytic anemia can be hereditary, you may be at risk if you have a family history of the disease. Another risk factor is the use of certain medications.

Diagnosis and Treatment

If you think you may have hemolytic anemia, see your doctor for an official diagnosis. He or she will do a blood test to find out if you have a low red blood cell count. You may also have to provide a urine sample, which your doctor will test for the presence of hemoglobin. In addition, your doctor may decide to do an examination of bone marrow and a measurement of red cell survival.

There are a few common therapies for hemolytic anemia. Your doctor may administer drugs; if this doesn't improve your condition, a splenectomy (a removal of the spleen) may be considered. Also, immunosuppressive therapy can be given if you do not respond to the other treatments. Your doctor should monitor your general condition and use of medications.

As with some of the other forms of anemia, treatment depends on the cause. For example, if you are taking a drug that triggered hemolytic anemia, you should stop taking the medication. Also, if you have a family history of hemolytic anemia, you should consider seeking genetic counseling before having children.

If you inherited hemolytic anemia, the disease is currently considered incurable. However, the symptoms of the disease can often be relieved or controlled with treatment. On the other hand, if you contracted hemolytic anemia (for example, by taking a particular medication), then the anemia can usually be cured. Scientific research into causes and treatment for hemolytic anemia continues, so there is hope for more effective treatments—and even a cure.

Chapter Five

Sickle-Cell Anemia and Thalassemia

As mentioned in the last chapter, hemolytic anemia can be inherited but can also be caused by other things, such as the use of medication. Up until this point, we have not seen any types of anemia that are caused only by hereditary factors. In other words, if these diseases do not run in your family, you will not get them. In this chapter, two forms of inherited anemia will be discussed. These types are called sickle-cell anemia and thalassemia.

Louise's Story

When Louise was young, she loved to go with her father to work. Louise's father was a doctor, and Louise loved watching him help people.

37

Louise thought that one day she would like to be a doctor, too.

But when Louise was in high school, she wasn't so sure she wanted to be a doctor after all. For one thing, she had developed an interest in other subjects, and she was quite good at them. She decided to ask some of her teachers what they thought she would be good at. Louise's English teacher told Louise that he thought she would make a good teacher, but Louise's math teacher thought she would make a good engineer! Louise didn't know what to do.

Louise decided to look into a variety of careers. One day after school, she stopped by the hospital where her father worked. Louise's dad was very surprised to see her there, but Louise explained that she was trying to figure out if she would enjoy the profession of being a doctor.

For part of the day, Louise followed her father around the hospital and watched him talk to his patients and the nurses. Louise was even allowed to participate: She helped take a young girl's temperature, and she helped the nurses with some of their tasks. After a couple of hours of helping out, Louise's dad told her there was someone special he wanted her to meet. He introduced her to a woman named Glenda who was lying in a hospital bed. She had had sickle-cell anemia her

People with sickle-cell anemia are often hospitalized for blood transfusions.

whole life and was in the hospital waiting to get a blood transfusion.

At first Louise felt uncomfortable talking to someone who was so sick, but Glenda's friendliness put her at ease. Glenda told her about her illness and about the procedure she was about to undergo. Glenda also told Louise that her father was a great doctor.

After talking with Glenda, Louise realized how important being a doctor is, and she remembered why she was so interested in the profession in the first place. She also learned that it is important to be thankful for what you have—and that even if you're sick, you can lead a happy, fulfilling, and inspiring life.

Sickle-Cell Anemia

Sickle-cell anemia is an inherited disorder that occurs mainly in African Americans. Normally, red blood cells carry oxygen to all parts of the body using a protein called hemoglobin. The red blood cells contain only normal hemoglobin and are shaped like doughnuts. These cells are very flexible and move easily through small blood vessels.

But in a person who has sickle-cell anemia, the red blood cells contain sickle hemoglobin, which causes them to change to a curved shape (sickle shape) when they are deprived of oxygen. Sickled cells become stuck and form plugs in small blood vessels. This blockage of blood flow can damage the tissues in the body.

Signs and Symptoms

There are many signs and symptoms associated with sickle-cell anemia. If you have sickle-cell anemia, you may experience episodes of severe pain, primarily at the joints, in the abdomen, or along the arms and legs; fatigue; pallor or jaundice; rapid heartbeat; susceptibility to infections; and delayed growth and development.

In addition to experiencing these symptoms, people with sickle-cell anemia may also experience episodes known as crises. Crises happen during the normal passage of red blood cells through the smallest blood vessels in the body (the capillaries). They cause the

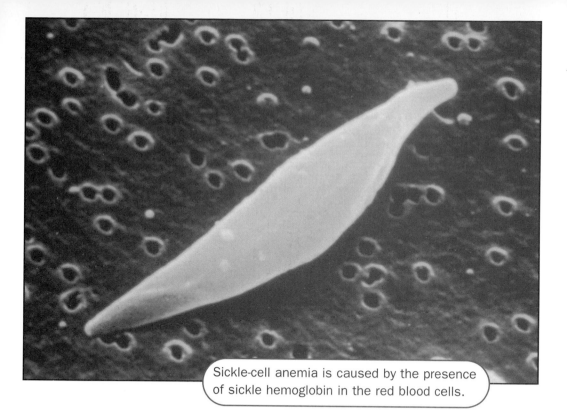

Sickle-cell anemia is caused by the presence of sickle hemoglobin in the red blood cells.

red cells to sickle, and they prevent additional oxygen from reaching tissues and organs. Crises can be very painful.

Causes

As mentioned at the beginning of this chapter, you will not get sickle-cell anemia if it does not run in your family. In order to develop sickle-cell anemia, a person must inherit two sickle-cell genes. If you only have only one sickle-cell gene, you have what is called sickle-cell trait. People with sickle-cell trait do not generally experience symptoms (except occasionally under low-oxygen conditions). They can also pass on the gene—and possibly the disease—to their children.

When both parents have sickle-cell trait, there is a 25 percent chance that their baby will have only normal hemoglobin, a 50 percent chance that their baby will have both normal and sickle hemoglobin (sickle-cell trait), and a 25 percent chance that their baby will have only sickle hemoglobin (sickle-cell anemia).

Who Is at Risk?

About 1 in 375 African-American children has sickle-cell disease. Hispanic Americans from the Caribbean, Central America, and parts of South America are also at risk for the disease. In addition, sickle-cell disease is found in individuals from Turkey, Greece, Italy, the Middle East, and East India. The overall incidence is 8 out of 100,000 people.

Diagnosis and Treatment

All newborn babies should be tested for sickle-cell disease. In some places, this testing is required. For example, in the United States sickle-cell screening of newborns is required in thirty states. The sickle-cell test requires a blood sample, which is taken from a baby's heel.

At present, no cure exists for this disease. However, with proper management, people with the disease can lead productive lives. Although therapy won't cure the disease, it can control the symptoms relating to crises.

It is important to protect an affected child from infections, which can lead to dangerous complications, including death. Because their spleens do not function properly, children with sickle-cell anemia are at great risk for certain serious infections. Thus, it is particularly important that children with sickle-cell disease get the appropriate vaccinations. They may also be required to take penicillin. Folic acid supplementation is a continuous therapy for sickle-cell anemia. In some cases, blood transfusions may be given.

What You Can Do to Help

Although sickle-cell anemia cannot be prevented, it is possible to avoid the triggers that can cause crises. For example, maintaining a good diet, drinking plenty of fluids, and getting regular exercise and sleep will help prevent dehydration and fatigue, and will keep the body strong. It is also important to remember to guard your body against infection. Taking care of wounds, practicing good oral hygiene, and getting regular checkups are all important steps in ensuring that your body is in good condition.

What the Future Holds

Although sickle-cell anemia varies greatly in severity, it is a serious illness for which there is no cure. The disease can be fatal during an acute crisis because of a severe infection or because of damage to a vital organ.

To guard against infection, it is important to take care of yourself, for example, by practicing good oral hygiene.

Sickle-cell anemia can be diagnosed before birth, so African Americans who are known to have sickle-cell trait in their families are usually advised to seek genetic counseling before pregnancy. In people with sickle-cell anemia, death from organ failure frequently occurs between the ages of twenty and forty.

Thalassemia Anemia

Like sickle-cell anemia, thalassemia is an inherited disease of the blood. Although there are cases in most areas of the world, thalassemia anemias are found most often in people of Mediterranean background.

The thalassemias can be divided into two main types: alpha (a) thalassemia and beta (b) thalassemia. Most people with alpha thalassemia have milder forms of the disease with varying degrees of anemia. Conversely, beta thalassemias range from having no effect on health to being very severe. There are also three classifications within these types: thalassemia minor, thalassemia intermedia, and thalassemia major. A person with thalassemia minor (also called trait) will experience no significant health problems, except a possible mild anemia. Thalassemia intermedia is an intermediate form of disease that requires regular care by a doctor. Thalassemia major is a serious disease that requires regular blood transfusions and medical care.

Signs and Symptoms

Most children with thalassemia major appear healthy at birth, but during the first year or two of life they become pale, listless, and fussy. They also have poor appetites, grow slowly, and often develop jaundice. Without treatment, the spleen, liver, and heart soon become greatly enlarged. Bones become thin and brittle, and facial bones frequently become distorted. Children with this disease often look alike.

Children with thalassemia intermedia, on the other hand, may develop some of the same complications, although in most cases, the course of the disease is mild for the first two decades of life.

Causes

This disease is passed on through parents who carry the thalassemia gene in their cells. If you have thalassemia trait, you are considered a "carrier." This means that you have one normal gene and one thalassemia gene in all body cells.

When two carriers become parents, there is a 25 percent chance that any child they have will inherit a thalassemia gene from each parent and have a severe form of the disease. There is a 50 percent chance that the child will inherit one of each kind of gene and become a carrier like his or her parents, and a 25 percent chance that the child will inherit two normal genes from his or her parents and be completely free of the disease or carrier state.

If the beta trait is inherited from both parents, it usually results in a severe, eventually fatal condition called Cooley's anemia. Children with this condition need repeated blood transfusions, which leads to the buildup of iron in the body. This buildup eventually results in damage to the liver, heart failure, and death in the teens or early twenties.

Who Is at Risk?

Thalassemia occurs most frequently in people of Italian, Greek, Middle Eastern, southern Asian, and African ancestry. About 100,000 babies worldwide are born with severe forms of this disease each year.

Diagnosis and Prevention

Blood tests and family genetic studies can show whether an individual has thalassemia or is a carrier. In addition, prenatal testing using chorionic villus sampling (CVS) or amniocentesis can detect or rule out thalassemia in the fetus. Early diagnosis is important so that treatment can prevent as many complications as possible.

At this time, thalassemia anemia cannot be prevented. A program of health education, testing for the trait, genetic counseling, and prenatal diagnosis can provide families with full medical information to help them have healthy children.

47

Therapy

Fortunately, there have been many exciting advances in recent years in the understanding of the thalassemias. Also, several new approaches to therapy have been developed.

For children who have thalassemia major, the use of frequent blood transfusions and antibiotics can be helpful. The transfusions, which generally take place every three to four weeks, are aimed at keeping hemoglobin levels near normal. If the hemoglobin levels improve, many of the complications of the disease, such as heart failure and bone deformities, can be prevented. Unlike children with thalassemia major, children with thalassemia intermedia usually do not require transfusions, although they may be recommended if complications start to develop.

One of the side effects of repeated blood transfusions is a buildup of iron in the body. Fortunately, an iron chelator can help rid the body of excess iron. Children with thalassemia major who are treated with frequent blood transfusions and iron chelation live twenty to thirty years or longer.

Thalassemia can sometimes be cured with bone marrow transplants. However, this form of treatment is possible for only a small minority of patients who have a suitable bone marrow donor, and the transplant procedure is still very risky.

In terms of diet, thalassemia major patients should

try to keep away from foods that are high in iron, such as red meat, liver, kidney, green leafy vegetables such as spinach, some breakfast cereals, certain breads, and alcohol. Your doctor will be able to suggest other foods and ways of living that can help maintain good health.

Chapter Six

Going to the Doctor

*F*rederique was terrified of going to the doctor. She hated getting shots and being poked and prodded. So Frederique wasn't happy when her mother told her it was time for her annual physical.

When Frederique got to the doctor's office, she had to wait a long time before the doctor was able to see her. This irritated Frederique, and she wanted to leave. But she knew that wouldn't solve anything, so she tried to wait patiently until the doctor was ready to see her.

"I'm sorry I kept you waiting, Frederique," said her doctor as he ushered her into his office. "We had a bit of an emergency to attend to, and we are a little short on help today." Frederique's doctor asked her some questions

If you think you may have anemia, see your doctor. Remember, he or she is there to help you.

about how she was feeling, and he did a regular physical exam.

Much to Frederique's surprise, the visit wasn't so bad. Sure, there was a fair amount of poking and prodding, but it's not as if any of that was painful. Frederique's doctor took a blood sample from her arm, but Frederique found that it was not as bad as she thought it would be. The needle felt more like a little pinch than anything. She even found that there were a few things she liked. The doctor took her blood pressure, and that felt kind of neat. Frederique was also happy to learn that she had grown a little taller since last year.

After Frederique got home, she couldn't believe she had spent so much time worrying about her trip to the doctor. She realized that most people probably don't love going to the doctor, but that it's not so awful after all. And it was nice to know that everything was okay.

The first step in treating anemia is to pinpoint the cause. Thus, it is important that you see your doctor if you suspect you have anemia. After you make an appointment with the doctor, he or she will talk to you about some of the symptoms you have been experiencing. He or she will ask you questions about your medical history and the medical history in your family.

Next, the doctor will do a physical exam and will check for some outside signs. This will help your doctor figure out what you have. Depending on your signs and symptoms, your doctor may decide to run further tests. Some of these include blood tests, urine tests, and bone marrow tests.

The important thing to remember is that your doctor is there to help you. Together, you can come up with a treatment plan that is right for you.

Glossary

amniocentesis Surgical removal of a sample of amniotic fluid from the uterus for analysis. This procedure is used to determine the sex or genetic abnormalities in the fetus.

biopsy Study of tissues taken from a living organism, especially in examination for the presence of disease.

blood transfusions Direct injection of whole blood or plasma into the blood stream.

bone marrow Soft, fatty, vascular tissue that fills most bone cavities.

cardiovascular disease Disease that relates to or involves the heart and blood vessels.

chemotherapeutic drugs Drugs used in cancer treatment. They contain specific chemical agents that selectively destroy malignant cells and tissues.

chromosome DNA-containing linear body of the cell nuclei of plants and animals. It is responsible for the determination and transmission of hereditary characteristics.

genetic counseling Counseling of prospective parents on the probabilities of inherited diseases occurring in their offspring and on the diagnosis and treatment of such diseases.

hemoglobin Oxygen-transporting, iron-containing protein pigment in vertebrate red blood cells.

hemorrhoids An itching or painful mass of dilated veins in swollen anal tissue.

infertility Condition of not being able to reproduce (have children).

jaundice Yellowish staining of the eyes, skin, and body fluids by bile pigment.

menstruation Process of discharging the menses. Menses refers to the blood and dead cell debris discharged from the uterus through the vagina by adult women at approximately monthly intervals between puberty and menopause.

palpitations When the heart beats faster than normal.

plasma Liquid part of the blood, containing substances such as nutrients, salts, and proteins.

platelet Minute protoplasmic disk, smaller than a red blood cell, found in the blood of vertebrates and held to promote coagulation. Without sufficient platelets, the blood cannot clot.

prognosis Prediction of probable development and
   outcome of a disease.
red blood cell Yellowish disk-shaped blood cell
   that contains hemoglobin and is responsible for
   the color of blood.
white blood cell Any of the white or colorless
   nucleated cells present in the blood.

Where to Go for Help

In the United States

American Autoimmune–Related Diseases Association
Michigan National Bank Building
15475 Gratiot Avenue
Detroit, MI 48205
(313) 371-8600
e-mail: aarda@aol.com
Web site: http://www.aarda.org

Aplastic Anemia Foundation of America
P.O. Box 613
Annapolis, MD 21404
(800) 747-2820 or (410) 867-0242
e-mail: aafacenter@aol.com
Web site: http://www.aplastic.org

Cooley's Anemia Foundation
129-09 26th Avenue, Number 203
Flushing, NY 11354
(800) 522-7222 or (718) 312-CURE [2873]
e-mail: ncaf@aol.com
Web site: www.thalassemia.org

March of Dimes Birth Defects Foundation
National Office
1275 Mamaroneck Avenue
White Plains, NY 10605
(888) MODIMES [663-4637]
Web site: http://www.modimes.org

National Institutes of Health
National Heart, Lung and Blood Institute
31 Center Drive MSC 2480
Building 31A, Room 4A16
Bethesda, MD 20892-2480
(301) 594-1348
Web site: http://www.nhlbi.nih.gov

National Organization for Rare Disorders
P.O. Box 8923
New Fairfield, CT 06812-8923
(800) 999-6673 or (203) 746-6518
Web site: http://www.rarediseases.org

Sickle Cell Disease Association of America
3345 Wilshire Boulevard, Suite 1106
Los Angeles, CA 90010-1880
(310) 216-6363 or (800) 421-8453
Web site: http://sicklecelldisease.org

In Canada

Aplastic Anemia Association of Canada
22 Aikenhead Road
Etobicoke, ON M9R 2Z3
(416) 235-0468 or (888) 840-0039
Web site: http://www.aplastic.ualberta.ca

Ontario Thalassemia Foundation
32 Fern Avenue
Weston, ON M9N 1M2
(416) 242-THAL [8425]
e-mail: thalassemia-ca@geocities.com

Vancouver Thalassemia Society of British Columbia
P.O. Box 38055, King Edward Mall
Vancouver, BC V5Z 4L9
(604) 980-3274

Web Sites

Anemia
http://www.adam.com/ency/article

Baby Net: Sickle-Cell Disease
http://babynet.ddwi.com/tlc/pregnancy/sicklecell.html

Disorders of the Red Blood Cells
http://cpmcnet.cpmccolumbia.edu/texts

Sickle-Cell Anemia
http://accessatlanta.adam.com/ency/article/00527

For Further Reading

Beshore, George. *Sickle-Cell Anemia.* Danbury, CT: Franklin Watts, 1994.

Kelly, Pat. *Coping with Sickle-Cell Anemia.* New York: The Rosen Publishing Group, 1999.

Lark, Susan. *Dr. Susan Lark's Heavy Menstrual Flow and Anemia.* Berkeley, CA: Ten Speed Press, 1996.

Tapper, Melbourne. *Sickle Cell Anemia and the Politics of Race.* Philadelphia: University of Pennsylvania, 1998.

Uthman, Ed. *Understanding Anemia.* Oxford, Mississippi: University of Mississippi Press, 1998.

Index

Index

treatment, 17–18
who is at risk, 17

G
genetic counseling, 36, 45, 48

H
hemoglobin, 6, 7, 11, 35, 40, 42, 48
hemolytic anemia, 32–33
    causes of, 35
    diagnosis, 35–36
    hereditary factors, 34–37
    other names for, 32
    symptoms of, 33–34
    treatment for, 36

I
infection, 16, 26, 29, 30, 40, 43, 44, 45
intrinsic factor, 22–23
iron buildup, 48
iron-deficiency anemia
    diet and, 12–13, 14–15
    symptoms, 11–12
    treatment and prevention, 13–14
    who is at risk, 12, 13
iron supplements, 33, 40
irregular heartbeat, 33, 40

J
jaundice, 16, 33, 40, 46

L
liver, 19, 24, 46, 47

M
megaloblastic anemia, 15
menstruation, 12, 13

O
oxygen, 7, 11, 25, 40, 41, 42

P
paleness, 2, 7, 9, 10, 12, 16, 33, 40, 46
pernicious anemia, 18, 19–21
    diagnosis, 23
    diet and, 22
    symptoms, 22–23
    treatment, 23–24
    who is at risk, 22, 23
platelets, 6, 26, 31
pregnancy, 13, 16, 17, 45

R
red blood cells, 6, 11, 16, 25, 26, 31, 32, 33, 35, 40, 41

S
Schilling's test, 23–24
shortness of breath, 9, 12, 22, 31, 33
sickle-cell anemia, 35, 37, 39, 40
    causes, 41–42
    crises, 40–41, 43
    diagnosis, 42, 45
    hereditary factors, 37, 41–42
    symptoms, 40
    testing, 42
    treatment, 42–43
    who is at risk, 42

About the Author

Allison J. Ross works in communications for a professional services firm in New York City. This is her second book for young adults.

Photo Credits

Cover shot by Brian Silak. All interior shots by Brian Silak except pp. 2, 26, 41 © Custom Medical; pp. 28, 39 © Index Stock; and p. 34 by Ira Fox.

Layout

Geri Giordano